AF416219

Contents

Introduction

California

I promise, you can create short videos like that too. Try to understand what makes you feel a certain way when you are watching something. It can be a picture, or a movie, or anything else. This will help you to cause those particular feelings consciously, in yourself and your audience. Additionally, learn to frame, exposure and according to that, control your camera. Both skills combined will give you the know-how to capture your own gorgeous movies. The video above consists of small frames which are bound together! Pay attention, every movie is build like that. We never remember every little detail of our last trip to France, or Italy, or the Bahamas. But a few certain moments will burn into our memory and eventually stay there forever.

Some will even become parts of our personalities. And exactly these moments are what you are searching for.

First, you have to see those situations and then capture them! Moments like that rarely happen when we are alone, but rather together with others we love, because they have the power to connect people. Allow those moments to happen. Try to see the big picture, but even more, the small one. Keep an eye on this small puzzle-pieces, they are all around us and sometimes they just stay for a few seconds.

For me, filmmaking is like playing music. You don't invent the notes, they are all there already. Like one of the biggest piano virtuoso and composer ever lived said:

All you have to do, is to play the right notes at the right time

The Beginning

The Canon 5D Mark II started the DSLR revolution. This camera turned the cinematography world around. Now you could shoot professional movies on something like a DSLR. Suddenly, shooting at low light due to the large sensor, or using shallow depth of field with 1080p/24, in short, getting professional quality images was possible for everyone. Well, it's almost true. Back then, when the Canon EOS 5D Mark II was released in 2008, it was the first EOS line camera providing video recording functions. Yes, there were DSLR's before which could capture video and even 1080p/24, which only became possible on the 5D Mark II through an official Canon Firmware Update in March 2010. When this Update finally came, the Canon 5D Mark II became the first full-frame DSLR recording 1080p at 24 frames per second. Independent filmmakers, Hollywood and even private hobby cinematographers went viral buying and making their own movies with the only full-frame DSLR shooting 1080p/24 available. This camera was and still is the groundwork for DSLR's being used in cinematography.

Why you should buy a DSLR?

Insane image quality and all this for near to non cost, easy as that! With the Canon and Blackmagic line you also have the possibility to shoot raw footage. This option starts normally at a price tag around $5,000. Raw is a file format which safes every ounce of detail and information which passes on your DSLR sensor. On the other hand, the regular video format (H.264) is compressed. You still can get good shoots, but loose tons of information along the way. This is especially important during Post-Production and grading. Here is an example of the difference between Raw and H.264. Additionally, the guy will explain you when you preferably should use raw and how.

Comparison between RAW and H.264 Codec

The large sized sensors of DSLR cameras can capture and handle low-light situations extremely well. Shooting at night or underwater becomes a child's play.

Paired with the right lenses, everyone can achieve breathtaking results in no time. Problems which appeared at the very beginning of the DSLR video era, like rolling shutter and moiré/aliasing (different signals become identical and cause processing problems), have been almost eliminated completely ever since. With the following cameras, you won't have to think about these problems ever again. Finally YES, you can shoot professional and gorgeous looking movies, all by yourself. Keep in mind though, even the best camera on this planet won't suddenly make you the next Steven Spielberg.

The DSLR, Camcorder, iPhone or whatever you use, is just your instrument to show the people your dreams, your perspective and ideas. Make other people dream, give them the courage to travel around the world, or pursue their particular goals!

Benefits

- You have control over the shallow depth of field, blur the background
- A Big sensor allows shooting in low-light situations
- It is portable, lightweight and can be used everywhere
- It costs way less money
- If used the right way, can produce professional quality video

Disadvantages

- The only reason is that DSLR's can't hold focus well on moving objects. Well they can, but not as good as their Hollywood counterparts.

The real voyage of discovery consists not in seeking new landscapes, but in having new eyes.

-Marcel Proust

Canon EOS 5D Mark III

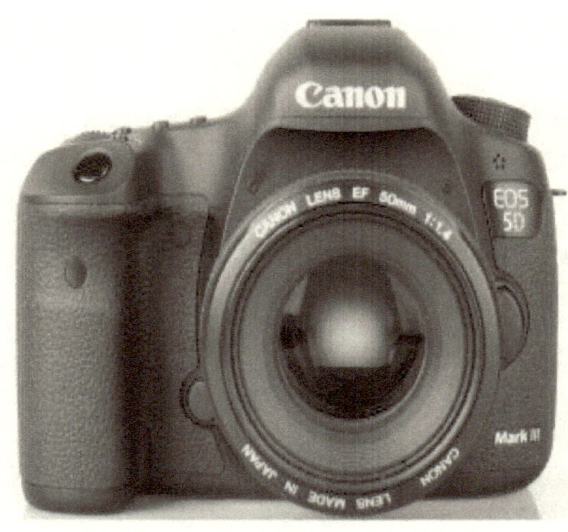

Simply the best in the business. Before we start, just watch this!
<u>Canon 5D Mark III, Girl Of My Dreams</u>

This is why cinematographers today are using this DSLR, because it produces these natural and marvelous colors. There isn't a competitor who comes even close to the 5D Mark III in this specific field, even among professional movie cameras, which are starting at price tags around $20,000. The new launched Canon EOS 5D Mark IV will ensure massive price drops for our 5D Mark III, which surpasses its successor in terms of price-performance ratio by far.

Additionally, Canon did an awesome job eliminating rolling shutter and moiré/aliasing completely by giving the 5D Mark III a built in Moiré Filter. The predecessor, 5D Mark II, and many other DSLRs had suffered from this problem a lot. Using this camera is intuitive, every button is where it should be.

The white balance access is easy and fast, the built quality feels like you can run through the Sahara with this thing, throughout using it as a pillow and still be sure, this 5D Mark III, no matter what happens, will work! Especially when you are traveling, you and your camera in the farthest corners of the world, it gives you a feeling of pure calmness and unconditional enjoyment. Finally, I think you already knew it, the Canon EOS 5D Mark III is the best DSLR for shooting in RAW. Just install MagicLantern, buy yourself a bunch of fast CV-Cards and you are set almost for life. The installation of MagicLantern is simple and it works 100 percent without any problems.

MagicLantern Firmware Update

Because the stock 5D Mark III can't record in RAW, you will have to install an additional firmware which allows you to do that. Installing the MagicLantern Firmware on your 5D Mark III is extremely straightforward, 100 percent safe and simple. Because it gets load completely from your memory card, it won't affect the guaranty at all. First, you will need a fast CF Card and the MagicLantern Software which can be downloaded here:

- Original Magic Lantern Guide

If you still have difficulties, here is an additional video for installing MagicLantern on the 5D Mark III:

- Youtube Video Guide

Recording in Raw requires much bigger amounts of data recording onto your CF Card, you will have to buy one of the following options.

1. KomputerBay Professional 128GB 1066x UDMA 7 (Best price for value)
2. SanDisk Extremee PRO 128gb UDMA 7
3. Lexar Professional 128GB 1066x UDMA 7

The 128GB and cards are working best with MagicLantern. I put the KomputerBay first, because it is the cheapest option and as reliable and as performing as the other two. Nevertheless, if you want the assurance and image of SanDisk and Lexar, go for it. All three will work without any problems.

Best videographer Lenses for your 5D MK III

Let's say it like this, a good lens means everything in getting the right shot. Your camera can only see through the objective you put on it, therefore the objectives are your camera's eyes. A bad lens on a good camera will rather produce bad results, whereas a good lens and an old body can produce very beautiful results. Here are the best lenses.

Note: One of the most important and lightly overlooked points in filming with a DSLR is the focus ring on your lens. It should move smoothly, without any faltering. Every camera in this eBook has top notch AutoFocus, but we as cinematographers sometimes, actually most of the time, need to have the option of going manual and adjusting the focus ourselves. All following lenses offer this without exception.

1. <u>Canon EF 50mm f/1.8 STM Lens</u>
   Best bang for the buck, shooting at night won't be a problem, because this lens is extremely light sensitive and can be used for almost everything! Prime lenses in general do not just offer superb image quality, they also teach you a lot about positioning and light. Finally, it's small and can be used perfectly for traveling. This lens is a must!

2. <u>Zeiss 35mm f/2 Distagon ZE</u>
   For video, there isn't anything comparable. Zeiss ZE lenses are one of the best. It has no Auto Focus, therefore you have to do it manually. But I tell you what, the richness of the colors, the projection and this throughout insane sharpness will make you smile, for years! I sometimes had the feeling that I don't even need any post production with this one. This is one of those lenses, where you can see the difference right from the moment you put it on. Some people on amazon described, it has an effect, like you can plunge into the image itself. This lens creates a depth which not even the best Canon L lenses could dream of. Without any hesitation I can promise, this paired with the Canon 5D Mark III will show you the full potential of this DSLR and produce breathtaking video shoots.

3. <u>Samyang 14mm f/2.8</u>

For Ultra-Wide Lenses, at this price point, comes nothing close! Even if we double the costs for this lens you won't find something better. Ultra-Wide lenses are all about expanding your image, they emphasize. What's close comes closer, what's far goes even further. They can create an experience like the viewer is actually standing on that mountain, in the middle of a desert, or running through an evergreen jungle.

Why prime lenses

Straightforward because they perform way better. They are faster, good ones have near to none distortion or vignetting and are crystal sharp. If you could buy just one lens, always go with the 50mm. Remember, if you decide to go with a full frame camera, then the lens you buy should also be designed for full frame sensors. Choosing the recommendations above, you are guaranteed to get the best out of your Canon EOS 5D Mark III.

The Best video Settings

First, you need to format your CF Cards into ExFAT and not Fat32. This will allow MagicLantern to record file size greater than 4GB. The 5D Mark III can't do that, therefore you will need a computer. Picture Styles, White Balance and digital ISO have no affect when shooting RAW, you can reedit almost everything in post production, anyways, to make things easier, keep the picture settings as flat as possible. Most of the time we are shooting at the cinematic standard 24 (23,976) frames per second, because it will make your shoots look filmic.

This is due to the way our eyes and brain process images. Exactly 23,976 successive images in one second create the impression of capturing the lightly blurred real life we experience every day. Additionally, we will have to adjust the shutter speed according to our previous chosen frame rate.

As a rule of thumb: Your shutter speed should be doubling the number of frames per second.

For example: 24p (frames per second) therefore we choose 1/48 concerning our shutter speed. Because most DSLRs can't represent the exact double, we choose the next possible number. For Canon this would be 1/50. But see for yourself, try different settings and observe how they affect your picture.

Camera Settings Checklist

- Focus on keeping the light behind you, this way the person, landscapes etc. you are shooting will get exposed properly.
- Your Mindset: Find something interesting you want to show other people and present it in a fashion, so that they think this something is the best thing they ever saw.
- Follow the rule: Your shutter speed should be doubling the number of frames per second.
- All takes you shoot, shouldn't cross the 10 second's mark. Every movie, or interesting video consists of short, intensive lined up shots. The person should get lost by the richness of detail and the overload of vast impressions. Keep them on distance, so they can't fully grasp your video especially watching it the first time. Tear them back and forth from the smallest, crystal clear details, to the most colorful and endless landscapes, create immense contrast!
- Finally, you have to tell a very interesting story to your audience. A bunch of nice different shoots that look just good, will do you nothing.

- You need a journey, a purpose behind this process. Read great novels, follow their story line, look how things develop, peak end and then rise again. This can teach you a lot. You have to move your audience. And always keep in mind what you are shooting and how they will see it.
- For slow motion or fast forward effects use Software, it just results in superior results.
- Go Manual. I know automatic focus can be cool, but not for us. Learn to control the camera first and built on that.

Examples of using the 5d Mark

7 Days in Europe
Film Festivals & Indie Films, The Overnight
Loving Lanka

Buy Your Canon EOS 5D Mark III Now!

Blackmagic Pocket Cinema Camera

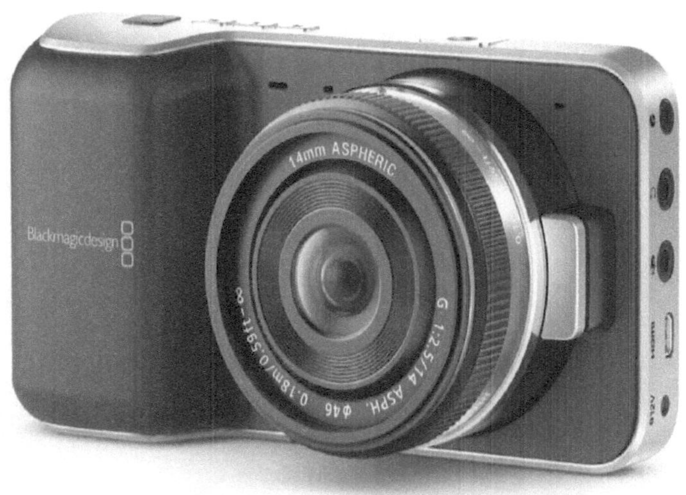

This camera has it already in the name (cinema).
Blackmagic Pocket Cinema Camera in Venice

Right out the box it records in Adobes beautiful Raw format, so called CinemaDNG. Additionally you can choose Apples ProRes HQ format, which simplifies your workflow enormously. The Blackmagic Pocket Cinema Camera produces terrifically detailed images. It's extremely portable, incredibly easy to use and designed for serious video productions.

You could go all out, rig your Blackmagic Pocket Cinema Camera, buy a set of handsome Zeiss Compact Primes, and you are ready to shoot your movie with Hollywood quality results. Keep in mind this camera costs just under $1000, count additionally some equipment and you can get one of the finest images today possible!

In comparison, Hollywood's darlings like the ARRI ALEXA series are starting at around $40.000.

But this baby also has some setbacks. Poor battery life, get ready to buy some additional batteries. The screen isn't the best, because it doesn't display colors accurately. Nevertheless, the material which comes out of this small compact hero is awesome.

Best SD Cards for your BMPCC

Recording CinemaDNG Raw needs speed. Therefore, you will have to buy a fast SD card. Make sure to get more than just one card. Which exact storage size you pick isn't important. Blackmagic itself is recommending to buy this:

- SanDisk Extreme PRO 128GB U3

I picked the 128GB version, because it seems most convenient for shooting Raw. Additionally, you can get a smaller SD card for separately recording ProRes HQ, requires significantly less storage space. Apple ProRes is a compressed codec, designed to offer high quality while requiring much less disk space than e.g. Raw. ProRes 422 is the default workhorse video format for all optimized media in Final Cut Pro X.

Note: Even if your camera only manages to do 8 bit video, it's still better to work with a 10 bit codec like ProRes, because all editing and processing will then be done at a higher resolution (H.264 converting through software to ProRes).

Best videographer Lenses for your BMPCC

The BMPCC is a Micro-Four-Thirds-Bajonett camera. MFT cameras are being used for documentaries that call for small, compact, highly mobile action and also for independent films wanting a true cinematic style. Not only are these cameras generally smaller and often less expensive, they offer more lens choices, longer shooting times, and greater depth of field.

Filmmakers now and then had a very simple choice when it came to the format in which they wanted to shoot, 35mm and 16mm. Big-Budget Hollywood Blockbusters are getting shot in the industries gold standard, 35mm, independent films, documentaries and travel movies most of the time are using 16mm. The simple reason is, because it safes money. The Micro Four Thirds system, with a sensor size equivalent to a 4/3-inch video tube, allows filmmakers to achieve a shallow depth of field that is cinematic, yet versatile. Shooting on 35mm or the digital equivalent sensor means as shallow and selective focus as possible, but it also means that keeping the image in focus can be a real challenge.

On movie sets, Camera assistants and focus pullers use measuring tape, place marks for actors / lenses, and are aided by digital rangefinders and other tools, all to keep the image in the desired focus. This was another reason 16mm was a popular alternative to 35mm, since the greater depth of field for the same viewing angle was easier to manage, especially for the above mentioned documentaries and small or one-person shoots. MFT cameras and lenses have that same benefit of greater depth of field, yet maintain a selective focus that differentiates it from small-sensor video footage.

Additionally MFT lenses can be shared across different brands like Lumix Panasonic, or Olympus, or Carl Zeiss, or Voigtländer and Leica. All this, without any adapters.

Here are the best lenses for the Blackmagic Pocket Cinema Camera

1. <u>Carl Zeiss Veydra 16mm T2.2, Imperial Cinema Lens</u>
   Your search for prime lenses for the BPCC has ended, Zeiss compact lenses from 12mm up till 85mm are the best here, period. Designed and developed from the ground to just work with MFT formats, incomparable build and glass quality. The focus ring is just a pleasure to use, smooth like warm milk with honey and butter.

2. <u>Sigma 18-35mm f/1.8 DC HSM for Nikon</u>
   Put three of the best prime lenses together and you get this one. This lens will cover around 80 % of all situations. Insane bang for the buck.

3. <u>Metabones Speed Booster Nikon G</u>
   This is why you buy the Sigma 18-35mm f/1.8 for Nikon and not for Canon or Sony, because with this adapter you additional can manually adjust the aperture of your Sigma lens, which otherwise wouldn't be possible.

1. That's the whole point. Cameras with smaller sensors can improve their performance significantly by adding the Metabones Speed Booster. The Blackmagic Pocket Cinema Camera has a 3x crop sensor, this means we have a 3 times smaller sensor than a full frame camera. Your speed Booster adapter will actually almost turn your little Pocket camera into a super 35mm sensor camera and additionally improve the sharpness, color representation, and light sensitivity of your Blackmagic Pocket Cinema Camera. Your Sigma 18-35mm f/1.8 will become 0.71x wider and, now comes the really nice part, 1 full stop brighter. So finally you get a 13-25mm f/1.2!!

Adding the 3x crop factor of the BMPCC and just enjoy a 38-75mm f/1.2 zoom lens with unparalleled quality image reproduction. Is the Metabones Speed Booster worth its money? You turn your $800 lens into something, which is worth WAY over $2,000. You get access to thousands over thousands of new lenses. And all this with a small adapter which is extremely portable, well build and lightweight. In french you would say c'est parti big time.

The Best Deal

Sigma 18-35mm + Metabones Speed Booster. This is the secret weapon of every cinematographer who is shooting with the Blackmagic Pocket Cinema Camera on a budget. This small setup will cover everything with stellar quality. One professional cinematographer from the EosHD community said that this would come close to a $47,000 + Tax cinema lens like the Optimo 15mm–40mm T2.6. One thing is sure, the image you will get will exceed the $15,000 Canon C300! Andrew Reid from the EOSHD community researched this topic and I tested it myself, because it seemed a bit weird to me, that a setup around $2000 outperforms a setup which is worth around $15,000. Nevertheless, it's true!

Examples of using the Blackmagic Pocket Cinema Camera

Yosemite BMPCC RAW
BMPCC Footage

Buy Your Blackmagic Pocket Cinema Camera Now!

Panasonic Lumix DMC-GH4

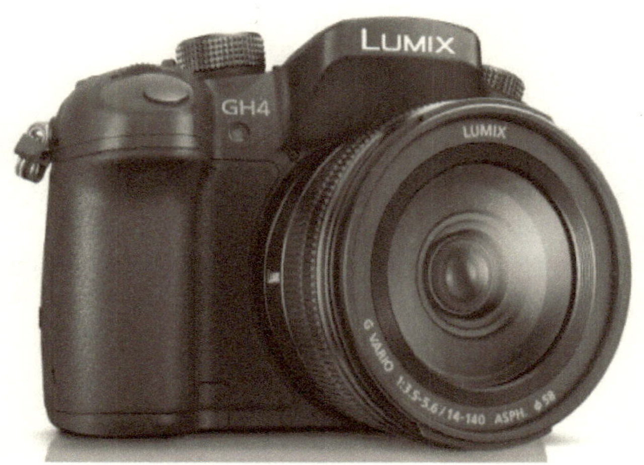

This list wouldn't be complete without this one. Before the talk, let's see some action.

Canada in 4K - Panasonic GH4

Cinema-4K-Resolution (4096x2160) in 24p is the magic phrase here. This mirrorless camera will produce the sharpest image of all here presented cameras. Keep in mind that in movie a bit of grain and blur is important to get it's natural look.

Besides plenty of adjustable settings concerning video, especially cinematic video, the main selling point here is the ability to take all the advantages of 4K and compressing them into the 1080p format.

Note: You also have the option to record Full HD (1080p) at 200Mbit/s, but shooting the video in 4K at 100Mbit/s and then converting it to 1080p will give you better results. Short, you get this camera to shot cinema 4K!

All this is supported by a Quad-Core image processor from Venus Engine. This speed gives room for the introduction of further updates and features. Panasonic is actually shipping a lot of updates, improving their GH4 even further and keeping everything up to date. Packed into a weather sealed magnesium alloy body, the whole thing just feels good and solid. You won't get the same richness of colors like in the 5D Mark III though, but in the right hands the Panasonic Lumix GH4 is one of the best cameras you will find out there.

Best SD Cards for your GH4

UHS Speed Class 3 SD Cards are the way to go here and this is exactly what gets recommend by Panasonic himself. Because you are not recording in RAW, these cards don't have to be that fast, but fast enough to ensure Cinema 4K with 100Mbit/s. Always keep a slight margin of air when it comes to writing speed.
This one will do perfectly:

- Transcend 64GB High Speed UHS-3

Best videographer Lenses for your GH4

Like the Blackmagic Pocket Cinema Camera, the Panasonic Lumix GH4 has an MFT adapter. Therefore, this time I will start with the best option to go here.

1. <u>Sigma 18-35mm f/1.8 DC HSM for Nikon</u>+<u>Metabones Speed Booster Nikon G to MFT</u>
There just isn't anything comparable to this setup for MFT bayonets. You are not forced to pick the Nikon version, it has its pretty big advantages though, but if you already have a bunch of Canon, Sony or whatever lenses, don't hesitate to go for their mounts.

   The math: 12,78-24,85mm x 2,3 crop = You get around 29,4-57mm f/1.2, Insane value for money! From here on it all depends on your previous choice. If you went with the Meabones Speed Booster for Nikons, you should find yourself a wide-angled lens, for the Nikon bayonet the next lens would be optimal.

1. <u>Nikon Nikkor 10mm f/2.8</u>
   With your Speed Booster and the GH4 you get a lens which will be at 16,33mm f/2.2, almost covering the important 16mm focal length.

2. <u>Panasonic Lumix G Leica 15mm f/1.4 ASPH</u> One of the best original wide lenses for MFT cameras.

3. <u>Panasonic Lumix G 12-35mm f/2.8 ASPH</u>
   Another MFT lens, great lens, many people are using this one as their standard lens. Nevertheless, this won't produce the same results as the sigma.

The GH4 is an incredible camera for its price tag. 4K will become more and more popular, even Smartphones today are starting to use screens that can display this resolution. Dynamic range though, will outclass resolution in terms of image quality. Raw recordings from the BPCC, 13 stops and the 5D Mark III, 14 stops of dynamic range. With the new arrived V-Log Update for the Panasonic Lumix GH4, they increased the dynamic range from 10 up to 12 stops, aiming to attract more professional videographers. Panasonic even claimed to be thinking about giving the GH4 the ability to shoot in Raw.

Optimal Video Settings

- Shoot in Cinema 4K! The IBP compression technology used there will produce the best picture in every situation for the GH4.
- Follow the rule: Your shutter speed should be doubling the number of frames per second.
- Keep in mind the Panasonic Lumix GH4 gives you a bunch of video controls. This camera actually was originally designed for cinematographers. As a result many people are messing around with all those settings and finally get worse results than just letting it on autopilot.
- Cine D and Cine V are your main workhorse settings. Both produce stunning results with a bit of tweaking. Use Cine D for low-light situations and Cine V rather for everything else. The following settings will work best and guarantee great grading results.
- Cine D Settings. Contrast: 0 / Sharpness: 5 / Noise Reduction: 5 / Saturation: 5 / Tint: 0
- Cine V Settings. Contrast: 5 / Sharpness: 5 / Noise Reduction: 5 / Saturation: 0 / Tint: 0

- Because the GH4 naturally tends to have oversharped pictures we approach this problem by reducing sharpness throughout. Noise Reduction can be managed way better in post production with for example something like Neat Video. Most importantly, keep your hands away from iResolution and iDynamic. Both settings will ultimately damage the image quality.
- The V-Log L Firmware Update, which gives you another video setting for your toolbox, can outperform the Cine D in higher ISO scenarios due to higher dynamic range, but will produce more noise meanwhile.

Examples of using the Panasonic Lumix GH4

Forever Young in 4K
New Zealand 4K, Aerial Drone and GH4

Buy Your Panasonic Lumix GH4 Now!

Honorable Mentions

Canon EOS 7D

Like on almost every Canon, you can install the MagicLantern Firmware and start shooting in Raw format. But the 7D is a sweet spot. Already used in Big-Budget cinema. Just to name a few:

- Marvel's The Avengers
- Black Swan
- End of Watch
- Like Crazy (entirely shot on the 7D)
- Act of Valor

Important to mention, we are talking about the first 7D, not the newer released 7D Mark II. Canons older version has, instead of one image processor, two slower ones, which however combined are capable of more speed, which comes very handy for recording Raw. The additional support of CF cards makes this camera perfect to use with MagicLantern. On the other hand, the 7D suffers a lot from moiré and aliasing, which fortunately can be completely cured:

Mosaic Engineering VAF filter for the 7D

Combined with the Mosaic Engineering VAF filer, you have a camera which can produce up to 2512x1052 resolution Raw files!

Yes, this will need some tricking around and the 5D Mark III can handle this way better, nevertheless, it is possible on a camera which was introduced in 2009 (the 5d Mark II is capable doing this too and was introduced in 2008). Keep in mind recording at 2,5k is not continuously, you will have maximally around 10sec (60 frames) for one take. Anyways, this body is going on eBay for less than $500, for some people who are just starting to get into cinematography this can be the real deal. As far as lens wise, go with a good manual 50mm, the Sigma 18-35mm f/1.8 again would be an optimal choice.

With the Metabones Speed Booster you can handle the crop factor of the 7D's APS-C sensor. And *voilá*, you have the cheapest RAW quality outputting camera there is.

iPhone 5s

Last but not least, something that nowadays almost everyone has. A smartphone. In this particular case, the iPhone 5s. On January 23, 2015, a film called **Tangerine** premiered at the 2015 Sundace Film Festival. Four days later Magnolia Pictures bought the world rights to this film. Throughout the year 2015 it has been released around the world and received a stunning 97% from Rotten Tomatoes, based on 129 surveyed film critics. IMDB gave 7.1 from 10. Metacritic 85 out of 100. I think you got the picture. This movie was ENTIERLY shot on three iPhone's! The starting budget was placed at $100,000. This thing box officed whopping $794,202. Now the big question should be, how? First of all, the iPhone 5s actually was the first smartphone which could make something like this possible. The slightly bigger sensor and wider aperture than his predecessor, gave the iPhone 5s serious filmmaking capabilities. In total, they used three tools to capture the image.

1. <u>Moondog Labs 1.33x Anamorphic Adapter Lens</u>
2. <u>FiLMiC Pro, ios application</u> Manual controls.
3. <u>Steadicam Smoothee</u> Jerk free recordings.

Here is an interesting interview about filming a feature on your iPhone with Sean S. Baker who filmed, edited, directed, produced and wrote Tangerine.

iPhone Filmmaking Advice by Sean S. Baker

I didn't say everything, but I drew everything
-Picasso

Finally, it's about the person behind the camera. Many people are finding their need to express themselves in their movies, or pictures, their music, or whatever direction they chose to go. It is a communication which can go way deeper than most people experience in their everyday life. For some of us, it is the only way we know to express ourselves. And we crave for people like that. Elvis Presley was naturally a very shy and humble character. Music gave him the chance of surpassing his anxiety, expressing himself and becoming a legend.

Brief introduction about 35mm and 16mm

Back in 1892, Thomas Edison and his employee William Dickson introduced the 35mm wide with four perforations per frame gauge. 1909 it got accepted as the international standard gauge and remained in that position way up till the introduction of digital photography and cinematography. This international standardization was one of the main causes why cinema could develop and spread around the world. Apparently, every country started using the international gold standard of 35mm and we had a uniform in producing, distributing and of course the presentation of movies. Cinema became a world-wide tool for communication and entertainment. To produce a film gauge was quite expensive, because the main image-forming compound was silver. This meant, the bigger the film stock, the more expensive it got. We needed a smaller film gauge, without loosing too much sharpness, or detail. Therefore, Eastman Kodak designed the cheaper, amateur 16mm format. It was easy to make and safe from fire, due to a new manufacturing process.

The 35mm gauge format transformed almost entirely into a
professional use, whereas 16mm formats are getting used by
documentaries, independent filmmakers and so on. This
classification remained to this day. Today however, almost
everything can be done digitally, with nearly no loss of
visible image quality at all.

CrashCourse Dynamic Range, Bit-Depth and Image Processing

First and foremost, we don't need to record more colors. Every normal JPEG already has more colors than the average human eye can see!
It's all about the depth and tone of the colors, this is what really matters. So let's say you capture an image in the JPEG format, the sensor processes the taken information according to your in-camera menu settings and finally safes this information as an 8 bit file. Most DSLR sensors today are capable of capturing at least 12, or even more bits of details. If the Megapixel Resolution describes your picture in two dimensions, how high and how wide it is, then Bit-Depth adds the third dimension, how dark or light every single pixel is.

Important to mention is, that canon sensors process information in a different way than e.g. Panasonic, or Sony, or Nikon... sensors. Due to this we get different results on different camera brands, even if they are in the exact same price range.
Shooting in compressed 8 bit formats like JPEG for photography and H.264 for videography isn't useful, especially if you want to work with your material afterwards in post production.

Further the Bit-Depth shows us, how many colors the camera can capture for every pixel. So a sensor which is capable of producing a 14 bit video can capture 16,383 tone values for each pixel. One 14 bit pixel can have 0 (black) to 16,383 (white) and 16,382 tones in between.

	tones per channel per pixel	total possible tones
8 bit	256	16.78 million
10 bit	1,024	1.07 billion
12 bit	4,095	68.68 billion
14 bit	16,383	4.39 trillion
16 bit	65,532	281 trillion

Therefore, 14 Bit images can display 4,39 Trillion different color tones. The average human eyes for example can distinguish between one million different color tones (trichromats), some few humans though can perceive around 100 Million different color tones (tetrachromats). There were hints, that people with these capacities exist, but it was never proven before. In 2010, however, a neuroscientist named Gabriele Jordan and her colleagues from the Newcastle University finally found one woman who was tetrachromat, she could distinguish colors superior to other candidates with ease. Owing to genetic conditions it is assumed that only women can develope this super-vision, but this talent needs to be trained and developed. Concetta Antico though, an Australian artist with studios all over the world is one of these women who flourished her gift.

The Dynamic Range is simply the limitation of the sensor in producing the whitest whites (maximum) and the blackest blacks (minimum). Imagine a staircase. The height of your staircase is the Dynamic Range (DR). Now we build some steps onto this staircase so you can climb it, these steps represent your Bit-Depth. No matter how many steps you would put onto this staircase, it wouldn't increase its height. But every little step will make the picture smoother, especially the transition between different color tones in your picture. Its like drawing a straight line. Every little point between your starting point (A) and the end (B) will make the line more precise and sort out any irregularities.

Keep in mind that a higher Dynamic Range will outweigh resolution in terms of quality at any time.
Let's say you bought the 5D Mark III. This camera has a full frame sensor which captures effectively 22,3 MP on 36mm x 24mm (sensor size), meaning we get a picture of 5760 (horizontal) and 3840 (vertical) pixels, resulting in a resolution of 5760 x 3840.
What happens now if we capture a video in 1080p (1920 x 1080) with 24 (23,976) pictures per second?

First, your camera has to quickly downsample the resolution from your sensors native 22,3 (effective) to approximately 2 Megapixel, which would equal
1920 x 1080 at 24p. Then estimate the true colors you have, or haven't seen with your eyes. And all this paired with the MagicLantern Firmware Update, in Raw!

Just keep in mind that this abundance of pixels (isn't beneficial on most cameras, because not just the pixel count, but also the pixel – sensor size relation is critical how information gets perceived), paired with the right processing speed and patterns, creates a true and crisp 1080p. Contrary to the vast advertising jabber, most cameras today can't produce a true 1080p.

Filters

Today, there are as many filters as monkeys out there. The ones you really do need though are Neutral Density (ND) and Polarizing filters. Polarizers reduce reflected light from surfaces like for example water. This is useful, if you want to get the deep rich blue color when shooting water, or the sky. Additionally, polarizers improve the contrast. *Note: Get a good circular polarizer.*

ND and Graduated ND (GND) filters are useful when it comes to control your exposure, especially during daytime. If you want to get some nice shallow depth of field during day time, you will need an ND filter. The GND on the other hand just darkens a special area of your frame, most used for darkening down the sky, thus balancing the exposure. There also are rotating ND and GND filters, which allow you to increase, or decrease the neutral-density effect. Useful when the scene you are shooting changes its exposure during the actual shoot, so you can rotate the filters and shoot without interruption (riding iris).

Equipment

Because I like to travel a lot, for me, buying a professional rig is nonsense. 22 lenses with 33 filters, for every situation imaginable, likewise. Some kind of stabilization is of course necessary, especially if your work will be shown on a big screen. I always tend to keep things simple, because this is when you can open your eyes, look around and find situations, which otherwise could get overlooked by all this clutter.

The only additional equipment you will need is a weather sealed, comfortable backpack and some good and healthy green tea, to keep your hands steady.

Post-Production

Very simple, I suggest learning to use software, which gives you the most freedom with the best results for your situation. The everlasting question between Apple, Linux and Microsoft really comes down to your personal preferences. For me editing on a MacBook Pro always seemed very natural and intuitive. Nobody wants his computer to freeze after 3 hours of hardcore editing. I can tell you that exactly this happened multiple times on my windows desktop machine, but not ones on my MacBook. Furthermore, drinking coffee while being able to work from a beautiful restaurant in Paris, is very enjoyable and one of the main perks of working on a Notebook. In addition, the Retina displays are producing very crisp and color accurate images. Final Cut Pro X for instant, is only available on macOS and is one of the smoothest editors out there. Especially if we are looking at rendering time and time line playbacks, even on old machines. The following two YouTube videos will give you a better understanding about this topic.

1. 4k Video Editing on a 12 MacBook
2. PC vs MAC for Video Editing

Workflow Examples

- **How to Edit MagicLantern Raw Footage**
  For converting MagicLanter Raw files into CinemaDNG,
  try RAWanizer on mac and raw2dng for windows. Mac
  users just follow the instructions displayed in this video.
  The workflow for the Blackmagic Pocket Cinema
  Camera will be very similar.

- **Panasonic Lumix GH4 4K into 1080p**
  First, you will need to convert your material into 1080p. After
  converting your Cinema 4K footage, which by the way demands high-
  end hardware you can continue to use the editing, grading workflow
  from the video above.

The Best Video Editing Software

1. **Apple Final Cut Pro X**
   Very straightforward, user friendly and at the same time
   offers immense capabilities. Big-Budget Blockbusters
   like the Curious Case of Benjamin Button were edited
   with this software. Further you will experience much
   faster rendering times than e.g. using Adobe Premiere
   Pro on your Mac, due to its perfect optimization.

1. <u>Avid Media (Film) Composer</u>
   This program is the industry standard. Most mainstream feature films are edited with Avid. The big benefits of Avid are multi-seat edits and shared storage space. It means, you could throw 20 editors, 10 producers, then 5 story assistants and finally 15 assistant editors on one project and they could work all together, at the same time, even on the same time line.

2. <u>Adobe Premiere Pro</u> + <u>Adobe After Effects</u>
   The following YouTube video will explain you exactly when and where to use this industry giants <u>Adobe Premiere Pro vs Adobe After Effects</u>. Adobe Products integrates nicely with its suit of applications. Using Photoshop for stills continuous to be very common in professional environment, but not necessary. Now comes the big BUT. Assembling shots on the time line drives me crazy with Premiere. No matter how fast your system is, it won't playback without delays. On the other hand working with Apples Final Cut Pro X, you get very smooth and fast playback, even on older machines.

The Best Color Grading Software

DaVinci Resolve, Blackmagic

Short, best color grading software out there. On top you can download a free version which has almost everything you will ever need. And last but not least, resolve offers a fully fledged, powerful editing platform.

Rendering Visual Effects

Pixar Rendermann

There are two ways of producing special/visual effects. For one, we have special effects (SFX). All SFX are done on set and in camera without any Post-Production. Gunshot wounds, stabbing people, actors make-up, costumes and so on are all SFX. However, today most productions are using visual effects (VFX), its much cheaper. You can greenscreen an actor to make him fall from a plane, or look like hulk. Generally, all visual effects added in post-production are VFX. Pixar Rendermann is one of the best VFX programs out there, completely free and used for a dozen of movies.

Best inexpensive Post-Production Set Up

You don't need to spend $4,000 for a hardcore editing computer + thousands of additional dollars for software. Like you could see in the previous YouTube videos, even an old MacBook can handle 4K editing with Apple Final Cut Pro X. Considering this, working with 1080p and Pro Res (you will have to convert your files to Pro Res if you want to work with Final Cut) will be a joy on any Apple computer!

1. Apple MacBook Pro
   This one is the sweet spot. Very good display, long lasting battery, compact and enough power to guarantee smooth and fast editing, particularly rendering. Cost: $1,199
2. Apple Final Cut Pro X
   Simple, clean, in short one of the best programs for video editing. If compared to Adobe Premiere Pro, which will be almost around $1,800. Cost: $299,99
3. DaVinci Reesolve Blackmagic
   Best color grading software for free.

For around $1,500 you will get a completely smooth, stable and fast processing post-production system. Not to mention that your MacBook is portable, ergo you can work from anywhere you want. The point is, almost every program can edit, grade and add effects, but some are just way more effective in getting a certain job done. Post-Production in general is key in making your footage look cinematic and professional. Knowing what you can do with certain shots in post-production will open you more perspectives and angles of seeing and composing your work.

Millions of people are tired of working their 9-5 job and wasting their days sitting in a gray office, with down hanged blinds, completing endless exel-charts. If you are one of those, this here can be your answer. Shooting video commercials, working for Model Agencies around the globe, creating stunning Lifestyle movies and sharing those with the whole wide world through YouTube, or working on a new feature film. The possibilities are near to endless, if you have the courage to go for it. But its more than that. It's about seeing what makes someone, or something special, beautiful and displaying those traits to others. Seeing those qualities in the first place will enrich not only your professional work but also every other part of your life.

www.ingramcontent.com/pod-product-compliance
Lightning Source LLC
Chambersburg PA
CBHW021401160726
47994CB00007B/3041